I0753642

Thomas Powell

Memorial

OF

THOMAS POWELL, ESQ.,

WHO DIED AT HIS RESIDENCE IN NEWBURGH, ON MONDAY, MAY 12, 1856,

IN THE EIGHTY-EIGHTH YEAR OF HIS AGE.

BY

Rev. R. B. Van Kleeck, D. D.

NEW YORK:
PRINTED FOR PRIVATE CIRCULATION.

1857.

CONTENTS.

LIST OF PLATES.

Introductory Notice.

INTRODUCTORY NOTICE.

THE following Memorial may need a word of explanation. It has been prepared and printed by request. Upon the death of Mr. POWELL, it was the desire of the family that I should officiate at his funeral; but my absence in the West, at the time, rendered it impossible for me to join in the sad and solemn services. The duty was well done by a younger brother, whose judicious and excellent Discourse is hereto appended. It has been thought desirable, also, to preserve, for future reference, and as a meet and permanent memorial, the obituary notice of Mr. RUTTENBER, with the addresses of Judges BROWN, BATE and McKISSOCK, and Mr. MONELL, and the other proceedings of his fellow-citizens, on the occasion of the death of Mr. POWELL. The whole is PRINTED, NOT PUBLISHED, for private circulation among the many friends of Mr. POWELL and his family, and it is humbly hoped, may not be without profit to those who shall read it, as well as for soothing and comfort to those who are more nearly afflicted and bereaved.

ROBERT B. VAN KLEECK.

FISHKILL LANDING, JULY 31, 1856.

Memorial.

MEMORIAL.

"Vanity of Vanities, saith the Preacher, all is Vanity."

ECCLESIASTES XII. 8.

STRANGE words are these, when we consider whence they come. They are from Solomon, who, in all his glory, as the world counts happiness, was the most fortunate of men. With every resource of human happiness at his command, amid the splendor of the throne of Israel in its palmiest days—a courted and envied Potentate, with all the treasures of human knowledge, and a higher wisdom, with untold stores of wealth—with all that could gratify the eye, the ear, or the taste, in social comfort, royal splendor and intellectual enjoyment—in the midst of all these, we see the royal preacher sad and serious, and sighing forth his deep sense of insufficiency and vanity. No one can read the Book of Ecclesiastes, which was penned by Solomon as the result of a calm review and large experience of human life, without asking earnestly, How can this be? If King Solomon, in all his glory—so wise, so rich, so courted—was not happy, then, "what shall the man do, who cometh after the King?" Where can happiness be found, and what is the secret of that deep sense of dissatisfaction and vanity which was darkly written in every line of the experience and writings of Solomon?

In considering this question, and attempting to solve this mystery of the inexplicable life of man, the dealings of God's Providence, and our own experience and observation, come kindly to our aid. We can never so realize and bring home the truths of Scripture, as when we have them illustrated in living examples, and can see them clearly reflected in the mirror of their experience, whom we have known in life and lamented in death. Such an illustration and such a mirror have been given to the citizens of Newburgh, in the recent death of their oldest friend and neighbor, THOMAS POWELL. He came to his grave "an old man and full of days," ripe and strong in the vicissitudes and the experience of more than four-score years, not a few of them eventful, and in trying times. His fellow-citizens, with one accord, did no less credit to themselves than honor to his memory, when they gathered in a sorrowing assembly, to acknowledge their debt of gratitude, and pay the last tribute of respect, to one on whom they justly looked as their common benefactor. It is no part of our design to dwell on and repeat the reminiscences or the details of his early and his business life, or the traits of character and many services which made the death of THOMAS POWELL, to the community in which he lived, a public loss. The spontaneous witness of a whole community, in reference to any man, when death has set its seal upon his life and memory, can seldom go astray.

There is an instinctive sense of justice and an impulsive sympathy, which is generally true as the needle to the pole, either in its censures or its praises, of those whose lives it has carefully witnessed, and on whose character and death it unites to pass its judgment. Viewed in this light, the family and friends of THOMAS POWELL have good reason to be satisfied with the verdict and the witness of his friends and fellow-citizens. There must have been a deep, true sense of justice and gratitude, which could rally as one man his friends and neighbors—which could call forth such a tribute from such men, (LAUDARI A LAUDATIS VIRIS) and close the stores and bow the hearts of a busy town upon a week day, while bells were tolling and fond tears were falling as his requiem. The record stands, alike of frankness, in acknowledging the failings, and of justice to the virtues and the services of the man "whom so many delighted to honor." The record of his life, and the secret of such a tribute and such sorrow at his death, may thus be briefly summed: small beginnings, patient industry, simplicity and economy—free from parsimony and meanness—stern integrity, so deep a hatred of hypocrisy as studiously and always to seem WORSE than he really was, a wise and prudent forecast, a bold, generous, unselfish public spirit, "looking not only on his own wealth and good, but that of others," and freely venturing his own that he might seek the common welfare. These public virtues were crowned by traits of truth and tenderness, best known by a loving wife and fond children, and loving and admiring children's children, and his whole active life was chequered and chastened by passing clouds of sorrow and adversity, by well-marked seasons of serious reflection, by a large and most minute acquaintance with the Word of God, and by distinct and earnest thoughts, and forebodings of the future and eternity. Those who looked only on the surface of his busy life, may not appreciate this, but all those who knew him well, and saw him in the bosom of his family, in his hours of solitude, and in his hidden inner life, will recognize the truthful lineaments of one whom they looked upon in life and death with various and conflicting feelings.

It is not, then, with a view so much to him, as for the satisfaction and the good of those whom he has left behind, that we connect his name and memory with the important theme before us. Without at all invading, then, the sanctity of private scenes, or tearing off the sacred veil which hides his failings in the dust, or bringing out to idle gaze the unobtrusive features of his active, earnest life, we may consider and improve some lessons furnished us by one so long and largely prospered in life, and now so deeply lamented in death. If his experience in life and death commend to us the truth of God, and the vanity of earth and time, should not his surviving friends and neighbors welcome it, and dwell on it, and ponder it, and seriously and thoughtfully apply it, in the earnest and exciting bustle of life, and the serious and solemn contemplation of their own part and prospect, in death and in eternity?

1. Then, let us endeavor to ascertain the secret of that deep sense of vanity and dissatisfaction which was darkly written in every line of the experience and writings of Solomon. It was not as the King of Israel, nor as the wisest of men, that Solomon had this deep and painful feeling; but as he was A MAN, because "nothing HUMAN was foreign to him," and as a partaker of the evils and burdens of our fallen race. It

is because he was A SINFUL MAN, in an evil world, cursed by the fall and sin, that he knew no perfect happiness; so that, as life rolled on and the circle of his experience was enlarged, and the resources of happiness were multiplied, he grew more weary and sad and sick at heart, and wrote on all his splendor, his treasures, his court, his crown, his large knowledge, his many pleasures, "All is vanity and vexation of spirit;" "Vanity of vanities, saith the preacher, all is vanity." In looking over carefully this Book of Ecclesiastes, we have a large and comprehensive view of human life, in its every light and shade, in every changing aspect, every new experience, from the heights of prosperity to the depths of adversity; and from the bright and buoyant hopes of youth, to the sad sinking of age and of death—on all are written, by the sighs and tears of the wisest of men, and by the unerring witness of the spirit of God, these few, but warning, world-wide, universal words of warning and of truth: "VANITY OF VANITIES, ALL IS VANITY!"

Now, how can these things be? Is it not a bright and beautiful world in which we live? Is there not much upon earth to minister to man in his happiness, to make him thankful to God for his goodness, and to stir him up to rejoice in his portion, and praise God for his many mercies? Assuredly there is much of this, and yet it was never intended that the good things of earth should be the proper portion of the soul of man, any more than that this earth is to be his home forever, and this short life his eternity and immortality. On all things here we see and feel the blight and curse of sin. For "the CREATURE," that is the whole creation, with man as its lord and head, "has been made subject to Vanity," and the more he has of it, to know and to enjoy, the more deeply will he feel, and the more readily acknowledge, that "all is vanity and vexation of spirit." This cannot be the case with those who have made but a short trial of earth, in its promises, or who have had but a small portion of its hopes and its joys. For in the one case hope lures the youthful heart and leads it on, and builds for it imaginary castles, and weaves fair visions of delights in the uncertain future; and in the other, the poor and afflicted are left to sigh in sadness over their narrow lot and scanty portion, and to feel how much happier they might have been if fortune had smiled, or earth and time had been more lavish of their treasures and their joys. But when a man has "lived long, and has seen good days," has been largely blessed, has basked in the sunshine of prosperity and the smiles of fortune, has amassed large stores of wealth, has tried and tasted the sweets of popular favor, and has attained to the place and the portion he longed for, for such to sit down sad and disappointed, and muse of emptiness and vanity, and sigh forth his sickness of heart and restless longing—which disdain and look down on a portion so small—and roam and soar at large, in quest of a better portion, nobler pleasures and more satisfying joys; this is a practical, real testimony to the evil of sin, and the power and wants of the soul of man, and the vanity of earth and of time, which not only the wisdom of Solomon, but the experience of the world, has confirmed. All experience proves, that the more man has to enjoy, the more he desires; and the more real and painful his sense of insufficiency and vanity, whether he has wealth, or honors, or social comforts, or pleasures, or any other form of earthly joy. In Alexander, after he had conquered the world, sitting down and weeping, because he had not other worlds to conquer, we have the true type of man, in his deep wants and restless longing. The higher he rises, and the more he acquires, the higher do his thoughts and hopes ascend, while ever before him Alps on Alps arise, and bear him on, and tempt his upward weary way. In Solomon, thus sadly musing over so large a portion, and joys so great and high, we see how little earth can do to fill the soul of man, and that without God and Christ and Heaven, "All is Vanity."

It was so in the experience of our departed friend. It is well known how full was his portion, and how large his prosperity; "how small his beginnings, and how greatly increased his latter end;" how much he was blessed in life with growing wealth, and home comforts and pleasures, and a life as free from envy and from enmity as most enjoy. If we mark the contrast between THOMAS POWELL, in his youth, with his brother JACOB, their only fortune in their energy and integrity, and compare the little lime-kiln at Marlborough, and the one small sloop from Newburgh, the scanty store in New York, and their small beginnings at Newburgh, with the THOMAS POWELL of the last twenty years—the man of wealth, and enterprise, and public spirit—his name floating on noble steamers, and sustaining well-established banks, great lines of railroads using the power of his large capital and financial skill, a valuable ferry,

Eng^d by J. C. McRae

[illegible] Lovell's Homestead.

a crowded pathway of the noble Hudson, his property for years, the town in which he lived enjoying the benefits of his forecast, his large capital, his generous ventures for her good; all these, with the rapidly increasing treasures of his own wealth, gave him a place and a position in the community in which he lived, which, as the world counts fortune, were greatly to be envied and desired. His residence for many years, its very site first chosen for its adaptation to the work of a dairy and a farm, and afterwards adorned and beautified, until it sat as a crown of beauty on the hill-side, and looked out on the varied scene which the noble Hudson and the Bay of Newburgh, and the mountains and fertile fields of

Dutchess, and the distant and enchanting view of West Point, spread out before the eye, from every window of his dwelling, and every point of his estate, with the comforts of his family (not unalloyed by change and sorrow and death), gave him "a local habitation and a name" which, with all he had beside, would surely have made THOMAS POWELL a happy man, if to be FORTUNATE and HAPPY were always one, either in the design and will of God, or the experience of men. And yet, in the midst of all this, his sufficiency, he was in straits. His own experience wrought out for him the problem of the vanity of earth and its utter insufficiency as the portion of the soul of man, so that for several years, in age and when alone, he has been a weary, burdened man, restless and longing, looking for something higher than the world could give, and turning from his full portion and his busy life, to ask for and to seek, "that peace which the world cannot give, and which it cannot take away." To those who often heard him speak of the importance of simplicity, of how little of large means any man can enjoy, how wealth brings with it its cares and toils, and other reflections such as these, will make their own application of his views and words to the subject before us. I well remember, in an earnest conversation which I had with him a few month before his death, I was deeply impressed by the different aspect which his outside character and his hidden life presented. I found him alone, and enfeebled by a recent attack. He seemed ready at once to enter on the subject of religion. I spoke freely of the vanity of the world, of the worth of the soul, and of his need and desire of salvation. Most impressive and startling was it to hear from such a man the earnest fear expressed "that he could not be saved." And yet he seemed to grope and strive, in earnest at least, and may we not hope, successfully, for the way of life and salvation. I esteemed it a privilege to speak to him "of repentance towards God and faith towards our Lord Jesus Christ," and to urge upon him the importance of earnest, humble prayer, and looking unto Jesus, in simple and humble penitence, if he would be saved. I saw him no more in life, but could not but regret the disadvantage to which he was subjected, by the want of early religious knowledge, by the power and influence of infidel associations in his riper years, and by the engrossing and enduring habits of a life devoted to the earnest seeking of the world, in its cares and its portion.

In this his honest, earnest testimony and experience, those who have tried the world long, and for whom it has done much, may read their own thoughts and hearts, and while with conscious sighs they own that all is vanity and weariness, and sorrow and pain, they may turn away from these, to seek in God and Heaven their portion and their rest. With all those who have had these feelings, as life and time roll on, they will be for them and within them, more real and more deep, a painful burden and inward longings, which can feel on earth no rest, and in the creature nought but vanity. Your own deep sighs, and earnest, honest hearts, look round in serious sadness on your cares, your toils, your treasures, your homes, your friends, your prospects, your portion, and write upon them all, what all must know and feel who are creatures and sinners, and mortal and frail, "that all is vanity [and vexation of spirit," and with the wise man you will take your stand, and look out on the pathway of life, and the grave and gate of death, and say with sighing and sadness, "Vanity of Vanities, all is Vanity."

2. This brings us to consider the proper remedy for this deep sense of vanity and weariness. There must be some relief, some remedy for wants so great, and feelings and desires so painful and oppressive. He who made man's heart and soul, did not create these longings and desires for nought. He would not by the vanity of earth, only raise man's expectations that He may disappoint his hopes; nor tempt and tantalize him with the offered cup of joy, only that it may be dashed and embittered with sorrow and vanity, with pain and death. Oh no, for "God is love." He loves the crea-

tures he has made, and man in His own image, as their chief and crown. He does, indeed, embitter earth for man, but it is only that He may raise his thoughts and hopes to Heaven; He breaks his schemes of earthly joy, but it is that he may seek his all in God. He does allow him to journey on through life weary and heavy laden, with care, and toil, and sin; but it is that he may hear the voice which calls him to his rest in God, in Christ, and Heaven. It was so with Solomon, who looking wisely at the various paths and scenes of human life, when God offered him his choice of blessings, he chose not riches, nor honor, nor fame, nor the life of his enemies, but made the high and heavenly wisdom, his sure choice. And thus he gained with it the rest, and has commended to us from the olden time the heavenly rule and the sure promise, which a greater than Solomon has given us, "Seek first the kingdom of God and his righteousness, and all these things shall be added unto you." For God's kingdom in the heart, in righteousness, and peace, and holy joy, is that which can alone give sweetness and sufficiency to any joys and portion here. They sweeten with the cross the bitter waters of the curse; they sanctify the blessings and the portion of earth; they lead the earnest soul to trace these streams of earthly joy up to the fountain of eternal love; and He who has made all else to be but vanity, invites the longing soul to find in Him its portion, its rest, its home, its peace, its joy, and happiness, and Heaven. It is thus the soul asserts its true dignity, and its higher destiny, when it refuses to feed on the husks of the world, and leaves its broken cisterns and polluted streams, to feast on the banquet of Heaven, and to drink of the waters of life. This deep want of the soul, is the voice and the image of God, rising, "soaring, longing, ever tending upward and onward, that it may be filled with the fulness of God."

That our departed friend felt the need of this great remedy, and was not thoughtless and reckless of death and eternity, we have from the lips of more than one witness. The Hon. Justice Brown thus gives his testimony. Speaking of an interview which he had with Mr. Powell some time before his death, he says, "As I went to take leave of him, I ventured to inquire if the near approach of death inspired him with any terror. He replied with his usual cheerfulness, 'Not in the least. I have long contemplated the event, and am quite prepared for it. I have outlived my capacity for usefulness and enjoyment, and have no longer a wish to remain. I regard death,' said he, 'as a necessary as well as inevitable event, the consummation and completion of the state of being which we call life; and I shall encounter, without apprehension, and not without hope, the change which awaits us all.'" To another, at a later period, he said: "After years of anxious thought, he had come to the conclusion, that he could not atone for his own offences, and that he needed a mediator, and hoped for pardon through his merits." He further said, "that he always made it a point to examine his daily life each morning and evening, and ask God for direction." Such views of death, of life, of the importance and necessity of prayer, of self-examination, of repentance and faith in a mediator, in order to the forgiveness of sins, if faithfully carried out, must have brought to his weary and anxious soul, after long years of worldliness and of delay, pardon and peace, rest and hope. His sorrowing family will find soothing comfort in these and other like expressions, which fell from his honest lips. It is no part of our object, nor would it either be just to him or faithful to others, if we presented his character for imitation in its religious bearings and relations. Those who knew him best have done full justice to his memory, as a man of business and of public spirit, a common, public benefactor. In our attempted portraiture, we rather hold him up by way of counsel and warning, as an illustration of the vanity of the world, and its utter insufficiency, even in large possessions, and every form of its portion and joys. When we think of Mr. Powell, so often chastened and afflicted in his life, and living in the attractive atmosphere of sincere piety, in those whom he loved and lost—especially that dear, sweet Mary who so long preceded him in the way of death and the grave—may we not hope that these lessons were not wholly lost, and that his long and weary life, and the many infirmities of his age, and his death, may have helped not only to convince him of the evil of sin and the vanity of earth, but also brought him, weary and heavy laden, to God and Christ, for rest and peace. But all this we must leave in the hands of God, and for the issues of eternity. "The day will declare every man's work, of what sort it is." "The Lord grant unto him, and to us all, that we may find mercy of the Lord in that day."

In this brief memorial, which has been written as a labor of love, for the soothing and comfort of a stricken one, who has for many years been my own friend and my father's friend, I am carried back and filled with memories of the past, alike pleasant and painful. The scenes of my childhood and youth, the graves of parents honored and beloved, "now passed into the skies;" the recollection of the friend of my youth, the lovely, gifted and lamented JAMES A. POWELL—the recollection of the many of the aged and venerable whom I loved and honored—the thought of the revered trio of village Pastors, where the pastoral tie is so honored and loved, one of whom, the venerated JOHNSTON, has gone to his rest, while the faithful, useful, earnest and beloved BROWN remains, with the quiet and unassuming, but learned and pious, McCARRELL; all these, with many other memories, press upon my mind and fill my heart, while I pay this loving, heart-felt tribute to the scenes and reminiscences of the Village of Newburgh.

That they should cluster round the memory of one who lived to be its oldest inhabitant, and came to his grave amid its sorrows and praises, is both opportune and appropriate.

In the busy, active life and lamented death of him who has departed, we may see another striking instance of the vanity of human life. His large possessions and his pleasant home, with all the beauty and sweetness which nature and cultivation could throw around it, had no power to save its inmate and owner from the ravages of age and disease, nor to ward off the hour and the power of death. He has left all behind, and all that remain to him now of what God gave and he possessed, "are a shroud, a coffin and a grave." To his heirs who survive, are left the stewardship of a large and solemn trust, golden opportunities of doing and getting good, and the same sure prospect of death, judgment and eternity.

We thus see Vanity of Vanities written on all the treasures, and comforts, and pleasant scenes, and homes of earth; and we may learn to prize and seek the power of that grace and faith which can bear up the spirit in sickness and in death, and dissolving the tender ties and enchanting scenes of earth, reveal beyond this fleeting world a brighter, happier scene, which no change can mar, no sickness waste, no sin disturb, no death destroy—but where a heavenly inheritance, unfading and divine, and a holy, happy home of rest eternal in the Heavens, invite the weary pilgrim, and fill and crown the soul, a thirst for God and immortality. May ours be the pathway of peace through the shadows of life, and the home of the soul in the rest and glories of Heaven!

Sermon

PREACHED AT THE BURIAL

OF

THOMAS POWELL, ESQ.,

OF NEWBURGH, N. Y.

BY

Rev. J. H. Hobart Brown,

RECTOR OF THE CHURCH OF THE GOOD ANGELS, BROOKLYN, L. I.

Sermon.

DISCOURSE.

"What man is he that liveth and shall not see death."

PSALM LXXXIX, 48.

MY BRETHREN: A solemn event has called us to this place! An immortal spirit has winged its flight to God! Its ruined shrine lies there! The great clock of human existence has marked a life gone by, and tolled a knell of warning! A mournful shadow is resting upon this whole community. There is an unwonted pause in the hurry of worldly business, while conscience from its pulpit in the heart, in God's name proclaims, "THERE IS A TIME TO DIE! PREPARE TO MEET THY GOD!"

Brethren: Death is a very ordinary occurrence. In some form or other we meet it every day. Men are like the leaves of some vast-spreading vine; some, just budding, are nipped by early frost: some, the worm destroys in all their growing beauty: others are consumed by the burning rays of the summer sun: a few linger on until they are chilled by the cold breath of winter, and then they, too, wither away and are no more. No age nor condition is exempt from death's attack. None of us can tell how soon his invisible, irresistible arm may smite us to the earth.

And yet, so repugnant to our nature is the thought of death,—so contradictory to the warm life gushing within us, that few persons realize that they are mortal. The young man is strong. He is sensible of no present weakness, and fears none in the future. He can scarcely believe that his vigorous pulse shall ever beat feebly;—his bright eye grow dim—his springing feet, that lightly tread the roughest mountain way, totter and fall on the floor of home—his ringing laugh give place to the tremulous tones of age, overflowing with life. Knowing nothing but growth, he does not care to think about decay and death. So he plunges headlong into the turmoil of the world. His heart beats high with lofty aims, and his arm feels strong enough to accomplish them. Riches, pleasure, honor dazzle him with their brilliance. His bark dashes merrily over the foaming waves of life. He runs the race of hurry, bustle and excitement. It does not matter much which way he goes, so long as exertion gives vent to his fevered spirits. He stands in his own strength, and does not think that it shall ever fail.

Then God begins to correct him with many sad lessons and bitter experiences. Plans, supposed so perfect in their arrangement as to be beyond the chance of disappointment, are frustrated. He is deceived by men. To his amazement he finds that even he himself deceives himself. Wealth and honor, which at a distance glittered like diamonds, he discovers are only dew drops, transient and fading away. Dark clouds of trouble thicken about him. Loved and trusted friends are taken from his side. And by the long shadows thus cast back upon his life, he learns that its evening will surely come.

But, alas! How often men fight against the conviction of their own heart. They endeavor to stifle their consciences. They shut their eyes to the grave, and blindly rush on. It is likely that nearly all of us here abhor the thought of death, and would if we could, willingly reject the truth which God in his Providence is ever teaching us, that this world is not our home, but only intended to fit us for the world to come.

But, brethren, what is death that a man should not think of it? or, that a Christian should be afraid of it? What is death that it should make men gloomy and downhearted? Is it not only another phase of life?—of life without the body, yet of life as deep and real as that which we now possess? Death is not an absorption of individual existence, nor an end of individual being. The candle of immortal life can never be put out. Death conveys it from one room to another, and simply places it beyond our sight. Everlasting life begins in this world. Death is only a temporary separation of soul and body, having no sting, no bitterness, but sin.

I make these remarks because so many people cling to old, dark, heathenish notions of death, and do not seem to know how full of joy and comfort the teaching of Holy Scripture is. There we are told that to depart and be with Christ is bliss. Can this be true if death destroys our being, or even leaves us in a state of unconscious sleep? Our dying Saviour promised the penitent thief, "To-day shalt thou be with me in Paradise!" What solemn mockery if the dead neither understand nor feel, or, if there is no difference between the righteous and the wicked dead! Is it true that the joy of those who sleep in Christ is not perfect until the resurrection? Death is only the dawn of bliss. But when the purified soul and glorified body shall be forever united in an eternal marriage, and be welcomed into the mansions of celestial rest, with these living words, "Come ye blessed children of my Father!" then the cup of joy shall be full to overflowing, and man shall know the bliss which now is incomprehensible, and not to be expressed. It is utterly wrong, it is unfaithful in Christians to be afraid to receive what the Gospel tells of death. Jesus Christ has brought life and immortality to light. His divine revelation has opened the remotest future, and has made us certain of being. It has made us see that the dark mists and clouds which overhang the valley of death, all arise from our own sinful hearts. Then by the great atonement on the cross made by the blessed Son of God, for all mankind, it dissipates these fearful and threatening shadows. If the

Gospel be true, and it is, what have Christians to fear in death?

I do not deny that there is a deep and unutterable solemnity pervading the regions of the grave. There our earthly probation ends. There we enter the ante-chamber of the judgment hall of God. Our lives are written in volumes. Years are the chapters, and days the verses. Death writes the Finis, and seals them until the day of doom. But believe me, death gathers all its importance from life. In itself considered, the moment of death is no more to be considered than any other point of time. This very moment—now, while we draw this fleeting breath, eternal joy and eternal woe are in the balances. Life thrown in on either side, will determine the result forever. This hour the battle of good and evil is joined. We may side with the one, and be more than conquerors forever, or with the other, and bind ourselves in everlasting servitude. Now, the gates of Heaven stand open, and all who please may enter there. Now, while we live must we make our salvation sure. Life is but a span long. Death shall soon teach us how short a span it is.

But I feel that to-day I ought to speak especially to the aged. "What man is he that liveth and shall not see death!" A man may outlive his fellows, and seem to defy decay and disease. He may stand for years like a giant tree in a forest, the sole remnant of a generation departed. But at last he must fall. Oh! my venerable brethren, do not let your long stay in this world confirm you in the belief that death is yet far off. Do not let length of days only root you more firmly in this life. It is a sad sight to see an old man tottering down the hill of life, trusting to the weak broken staff of earthly support. But what vision is given to mortal more beautiful than of some aged saint—some Simeon or Anna—who walks in faith, leaning upon the promises of God. Old age unblessed by God! What a cold and cheerless thought. What is it like? It is a field barren and deserted. It is a tree rotten and without fruit—a ruined house—a glorious temple with its altar overturned and its columns broken. Oh! how ought hoary heads to be venerable, as for many years, so for many good works—for wisdom, faith, hope and love. The wheat is golden when it is ripe—the rays of the setting sun are soft and rich—and so the aged Christian shines in brightest glory when he stands on the brink of time, cheerfully and undauntedly watching the approach of the angel of Death.

My Brethren: I wish that other lips than mine were to speak to you of him whose body we are about to consign to the tomb. Your beloved Rector could speak to you in fit terms of one whose whole life was inwoven with the growth and prosperity of Newburgh. Most of you who now hear me could say with truth, that Mr. THOMAS

Powell went among men for an old man, in the days of your youth. Eighty-seven years sum up the time of his pilgrimage on earth—years which have seen the birth and vast increase of this mighty Nation, and the rise and fall of foreign Empires—years which stand thick with events of more wide importance. Mr. Powell was born in Hempstead, Long Island. When he was twelve years of age, his father died. At once the boy was compelled to grapple with the hard world. How successfully he battled is sufficiently shown by the very prominent position, as a landholder and man of wealth, which he held at the time of his decease. Having reached his eighteenth year, he came to Orange County, and from that time his life is identified with the history of this locality. I will not stay now to enumerate the different enterprises with which, at some time or other, he was connected. A man of untiring perseverance of purpose, of unusual energy and activity of both mind and body, possessing keen perceptive powers, with a large share of prudence, he could hardly help succeeding in whatever he undertook. Yet while prosecuting vigorously his own private business, he gave an impulse for good to the whole community. He did not confine his efforts to mere selfish ends. He was a true citizen, and labored to improve and beautify the home of his choice. With wise foresight and high liberality he endeavored to make Newburgh become, what its situation demands, a pleasant abiding place, a delight to the eye of the traveler, and a bright ornament of the State. His death is a public loss. He has indeed left a vacancy which cannot easily be filled. So many were the ties which bound him to this town and county, ties which, in the lapse of years grew stronger rather than weaker, that their sudden and complete disruption cannot but cause universal trouble and grief. There is a head and father gone from the people. Surely it is a time to be silent, and to commune with God. It is no more than right that to-day your business is suspended, and an unusual quiet betokens the deep respect which is felt for the memory of the departed.

I have spoken of Mr. Powell as he appeared to society at large. Those who shared his heart and his home knew him better than the outside world. They recognized and felt those kindly characteristics of his nature and disposition which smoothed and sweetened private life. As a father and a friend he was deeply and tenderly loved. He has left a stricken household. There are mourners who cannot tell the grief that burdens their breasts. But let me not rudely lift the sacred veil of private woe. God the Holy Ghost, the blessed Comforter, who left his bright abode in Heaven to dwell with man, He alone can speak "effectual words of peace and hope," words not to be heard, but felt.

My Brethren: As we stand here around the body of our friend, a solemn thought is pressing at our hearts. He has gone to his Creator and Judge! When we think of the vast issues pending upon the sentence which that Judge shall utter—a sentence which shall come with power, power that cannot be resisted—it is well that we know God is merciful as well as just; else our hearts would sink with fear. It is well that we know God himself shall be our Judge. Who else but the All-wise One could weigh the difference in physical and mental endowments—the powerful influence of early education, and the wonderful pressure of surrounding circumstances of life, circumstances which a man may not choose for himself, but into which he is inducted whether he will or whether he will not. It is enough for us to compare outward actions with an outward law. Even then we find it hard enough to be truly just. But the heart God alone can judge. All glory be to Him that he has revealed to us that great principle of His merciful equity, that he will judge a man according to that which he has, and not according to that which he has not.

Brethren, the death of Mr. POWELL teaches us that the longest life will surely end. It warns you, and it warns me, not to flatter ourselves with the certainty of human life. It warns us now, while we live, to acknowlegde and realize the intrinsic greatness of our nature, and the everlastingness of our existence. It warns us to turn at once, with all our hearts, to God. There is no man that shall not see death! Not many of us here present can expect to live to be old. Our sun may go down while it is yet noon. Yet if we accept reconciliation with God in the Beloved One, we have nothing to fear. When the shadows of death close around us, the dew of peace shall softly fall. The Star of Hope shall shine out. The staff of Almighty strength shall be in our hands. God giveth songs in the night! The darkness is no darkness with Him. In His light we shall see light.

A few more words and I have done. My brethren, God has given us time so that we may do all the work that He has prepared for us. We must work with fear and trembling, if we wish to be saved. God desires to be glorified in us by our faith and obedience, and by our brotherly love. Therefore I most earnestly entreat those among you who are careless of God's laws, to think that however great you may imagine your faith to be, if it does not produce in you the fruit of good living, it is a dead and profitless faith. While you have life, repent and amend your ways! I say it with all due thoughtfulness, that no man that knows God's will can blamelessly remain unbaptised, nor keep away from the table of the Lord, nor be negligent of the public duties of piety, nor be careless of private prayer, or any other means of grace. No man without peril to his soul, can be dishonest in his daily transactions, nor harsh, nor cruel, nor vindictive, nor covetous. In the Book of Proverbs, it is written: "The sleep of a laboring man is sweet, whether he has eaten little or much." So, the rest of a working Christian is sweet, whether he has been rich or poor, honored or unknown. "Blessed are the dead who die in the Lord: even so, saith the Spirit, for they rest from their labors." Brethren, shall such blessedness be yours? Shall such rest be yours?

Obituary Addresses

ON THE

OCCASION OF THE DEATH

OF

THOMAS POWELL, ESQ.,

OF NEWBURGH, N. Y.

DEATH OF THOMAS POWELL, ESQ.

THE following OBITUARY NOTICE appeared in the Newburgh Telegraph of May **15, 1856.**

THOMAS POWELL, ESQ., whose name has been identified with the business of Newburgh for some sixty years, and is as "familiar as household words" in every hamlet and farm-house in this section of country, as well as known and respected in commercial circles throughout this and adjoining States, died at his residence in this Village, at quarter past 5 P. M., on Monday last, in the 88th year of his age. For some time past, Mr. POWELL has been gradually declining. His last illness was from the 26th ult., since which time he had been confined to his room. Life's duties all performed, and surrounded by sympathising friends, he passed quietly and peacefully to "that bourne from whence no traveler returns."

The Powell family was originally from Wales. Their

immigration to this country dates back to the period of the possession of New York by the Dutch. Jacob and Thomas Powell were the sons of Henry Powell, of Hemstead, L. I., who, although at one time in affluent circumstances, was reduced to poverty by the vicissitudes of the War of Independence ; and who died when Jacob was 16 and Thomas 12 years of age, leaving them utterly helpless, with the care of a widowed mother. With that energy which ever after distinguished them, they grappled manfully with adversity; and the lessons which they learned then were their best capital in the active duties of life.

In 1788, Thomas and Jacob, in company with their mother, removed to the County of Orange, and settled near Washingtonville, where their industry led to some increase of property. In 1791, they removed to Marlborough, Ulster County, where the brothers opened a small store and erected some lime kilns, and engaged successfully in the production and sale of lime. In the spring of 1798, they removed to New York, and engaged in mercantile business, but, being driven away by yellow fever the succeeding summer, took up their residence temporarily at Newburgh. The Village was then small. A single dock and a store or two transacted all the business of the place. But the Powells saw, at a glance, the future. A comparatively large commerce with the West made Newburgh the head of its land transit, and the axe was already ringing in the forests, and the rich lands of Orange and Ulster yielding those fruits which pointed out the ultimate importance of the place; and they engaged at once in the mercantile and freighting business, and in the purchase of lands. As a natural consequence of energy and integrity, accompanied by the rapid growth of the Village, they became wealthy.

In 1807, while the Powells were busy with their sloops in conveying to market the produce of the rich agricultural district by which we are surrounded, the wheels of Fulton's boat, the CLAREMONT, ruffled the waters of the Newburgh Bay, and opened to them new ideas of the future, and with no little interest did they watch the development of that mighty agency which Fulton had discovered. In 1823, Jacob died, and Thomas succeeded to the business, and continued in its successful prosecution. In 1834, we believe, he built the HIGHLANDER, one of the most substantial and rapid steamers of her time. In 1846, he built the THOMAS POWELL, a steamer of remarkable speed. Both steamers still navigate the Hudson. Steamers for freighting purposes, however, were soon superseded by barges, and Mr. POWELL was first in placing upon the Newburgh line the NEWBURGH, and later the SUSQUEHANNA, barges which have no superior on the river.

Of late years Mr. POWELL did not take an active part in business, but his name and capital were successfully wielded by his associates, Mr. RAMSDELL and Mr. MOORE. He continued, however, to take a deep interest in his old pursuits, and was daily at his place of business. With that prudent foresight which always accompanied his transactions, one of his recent acts was to renew his articles of co-partnership, for a term of years, with Mr. RAMSDELL and Mr. MOORE, for the purpose of continuing the name and business of the firm without interruption after his death. Fortunate it is for the interests of Newburgh that the mantle of the Patriarch has fallen upon successors of such enterprise and ability.

We have only briefly glanced at Mr. POWELL'S connection with the business and growth of Newburgh. Although we have given prominence to the freighting interests so long under his charge, it should not be inferred that that interest received his attention exclusively. Identifying his own interests with those of the Village, a large portion of his revenues were directed to its development and prosperity. He was a large stockholder in manufacturing enterprises, in the building of Rail and Plank Roads, and his name or capital were constantly employed in mercantile and mechanical channels, and his hand moved behind the curtain and sustained enterprises which are now permanent and beneficial. All who remember the blighting effect of the construction of the Hudson and Delaware Canal, and later, of the New York and Erie Railroad, upon the prosperity of Newburgh, will never fail to acknowledge the promptness with which Mr. POWELL came forward and took the lead in the effort to overcome the disadvantages under which we labored.

Foremost in all public enterprises, the name of THOMAS POWELL is written in living characters on every page of our local history and progress. Whatever we are to-day, in a commercial point of view—whatever of prosperity and enterprise animates the public pulse of our Village—is due, in a great measure, to him. His large landed interests, his Docks and Store-houses, his Steamers, Barges and Ferry, the Bank that bears his name, and the noisy clatter of the Loom and Spindle, and the ringing whistle of the Locomotive which sound in our ears, are monuments of his worth. Newburgh mourns his loss as that of a father who has contributed indulgently to the happiness and prosperity of his children.

From the manner in which Mr. POWELL acquired and employed his wealth, we might draw lessons for example alike to the poor and to the wealthy. No one lives to himself alone. The means employed to secure wealth—industry, frugality and honesty—are open to all. The disposition of wealth should be, while promoting the interests of the possessor, to benefit those who may fall within the circle of its influence. Such was the conduct of Mr. POWELL. More than once did he stake his entire wealth for the prosperity of those by whom he was surrounded; and, as the noble ship breasting the sea dashes the foam and spray over all around her, so did he scatter prosperity, through his enterprise, in the community of which he formed a part.

In private life, as in all his transactions with men, honesty, integrity, and liberality marked the conduct of THOMAS POWELL. His was the "hand that scattereth yet increaseth." To private and public charities his ear was ever open, and none were turned empty away. Eccentric in some respects, he nevertheless carried with him a warm heart and a philanthropic spirit; and in his last hours "troops of good deeds, like angels, thronged about his couch, and buoyed him safely up when on the threshold of another world." The good he has done will live long after his name has passed from the memory of man, and rise in sweet incense to Him in whose presence "Charity covereth a multitude of sins."

"No longer seek his merits to disclose,
Nor draw his frailties from their dread abode,
There they alike in trembling hope repose—
The bosom of their father and their God."

Resolutions of the Board of Trustees.

At a special meeting of the Board of Trustees of the Village of Newburgh, held at the Clerk's Office, on Tuesday evening, May 13th, the following Preamble and Resolutions were presented by Mr. Kerr, and adopted unanimously:

Whereas, It has pleased Almighty God to remove from among us our venerable fellow-citizen, Thomas Powell, justly regarded as one of the Fathers of Newburgh ; and

Whereas, This entire community in his decease mourns the loss of one who has been identified with its best interests for more than half a century ; therefore

Resolved, That the members of this Board, as a testimony of respect, will attend the funeral of the de-

Funeral Services.

The Funeral Services of the late Mr. THOMAS POWELL, were attended, on Thursday afternoon last, by a large concourse of people. Flags were kept at half-mast during the day, and at the hour appointed for the funeral ceremonies, the stores and places of business were generally closed. The services were conducted by Rev. Hobart Brown, of Brooklyn, Rev. T. Riley, of New Windsor, and Rev. Dr. Forsyth, of Newburgh. A forcible discourse was delivered by Rev. Mr. Brown, from the text: "No man liveth on the earth and dieth not." The Reverend speaker, after an appropriate and touching enforcement of this Scriptural truth, called attention to the remarkable character of the deceased, showing in striking representation the strong points of his manhood—his vigorous mind—his untiring industry—his excellent business habits; and in all presenting his career as an example for the young men of the country. One of the largest processions ever witnessed ceased, and wear the usual badge of mourning for thirty days.

Resolved, That the citizens be requested to close their places of business on Thursday, the 15th inst., from three o'clock to five o'clock, P. M.

Resolved, That the foregoing be entered upon the Minutes, and a copy thereof transmitted by the Clerk to the family of Mr. POWELL.

W. L. F. WARREN, President.

CHAS. HALSTEAD, JUN., Clerk.

THOMAS POWELL
BORN FEB. 21ST 1769
DEPARTED THIS LIFE MAY 12
AGED 87 YEARS.

in this Village, accompanied the remains to the grave, under the solemn tolling of the Church bells—the following gentlemen acting as pall-bearers :

GEORGE CORNWELL,	SAMUEL WILLIAMS,
HENRY WYCKOFF,	URIAH LOCKWOOD,
SAMUEL JOHNSON,	SAMUEL W. EAGER,
BENJAMIN CARPENTER,	HENRY WALSH.

The impressive service of the Episcopal Church was read at the grave, and the body of THOMAS POWELL committed, "Earth to earth, ashes to ashes, dust to dust."

Proceedings of Public Meeting.

On Monday morning last, the following Call was posted in the streets of our Village:

Public Meeting.—The citizens of Newburgh are respectfully invited to attend a Public Meeting, to be held at the Court House, on Monday afternoon, the 19th instant, at 5 o'clock, to pay a tribute of respect to the memory of the late Thomas Powell.

JOHN W. BROWN,
DAVID W. BATE,
BENJ. CARPENTER,
ENOCH CARTER,
C. F. BELKNAP,
WM. C. HASBROUCK,
THOMAS McKISSOCK,
GEORGE CORNWELL,
E. W. FARRINGTON,
SAMUEL W. EAGER,
P. CHAPMAN,
JOHN J. MONELL,
THOMAS GEORGE,
HENRY WALSH.

Dated May 17, 1856.

At the hour named, the citizens assembled at the Court Room, when the Hon. D.

W. BATE called the Meeting to order, and nominated Hon. JOHN W. BROWN, of the Supreme Court, for Chairman. The motion was seconded by Mr. BENJAMIN CARPENTER, and was carried. On motion of Mr. GEORGE CORNWELL, Mr. E. W. FARRINGTON, was made Vice-Chairman; and on motion of Mr. C. F. BELKNAP, the Chair appointed Mr. BELKNAP and Mr. S. R. VAN DUZER, Secretaries.

Mr. BROWN then arose and said:

This Meeting has been assembled that the citizens of Newburgh might testify their respect for the memory of their deceased townsman, the late Mr. THOMAS POWELL. We, who have known him for so many years, who have been accustomed to meet and salute him almost daily, and who have not yet become reconciled to miss him from his usual places of resort—we who have witnessed his industry, his perseverance and energy, and shared largely in the results of his liberality—desire to express publicly our deep regret at his death, and our high appreciation of the manly qualities which distinguished his character. This is a mournful, but a grateful task. For, in doing homage to the memory of departed worth, we hold it up to others as a model worthy of imitation, and offer the strongest as well as the noblest incentive to the cultivation and exercise of that moral excellence which is the chief ornament of our nature, and which ensures the happiness and progress of our race. The character and tendencies of the individual mind, depend somewhat upon external influences and the circumstances by which the individual is surrounded. The Athenian of the age of Pericles; the Roman of that of Brutus; the Briton who lived in the time of the Cromwells, the Vanes and the Hampdens; and the Anglo-American of the time of the Washingtons, the Hancocks and the Franklins, could hardly fail to find the character of his mind affected, and his faculties enlarged and invigorated, by the events of which he was a constant spectator. In great emergencies, the public interests are everything—those of the individual absolutely nothing It is then that men forget themselves and all that concerns them as individuals, in their efforts to accomplish great objects—to establish great principles—perchance to preserve their country from conquest and subjugation, or in the hope of investing its history with the halo of imperishable renown. These are the true heroic ages—periods which shed the light of heroic action far into the vista of future times, and exhibit for the instruction and imitation of posterity, the noblest examples of courage and constancy—of self-denial and public virtue.

It was in one of these eventful eras that Mr. POWELL began the career of life—an era fruitful of great events—prolific of great men. He was just seven years of age when the Revolutionary struggle began, and saw and remembered some of the conflicts of arms and opinion which preceded and were consummated in the establishment of the National Independence. He connected the present with the Revolutionary age, and was among the few last remnants of a generation now no more. Who shall say what power and energy the stirring scenes of his early youth may have imparted to his strong and vigorous mind? Who shall undertake to determine how much of that fortitude and moral courage—how much of that force and fidelity of purpose which distinguished his character, may have been inspired by the illustrious examples by which his early manhood was surrounded?

Mr. POWELL had his faults and his eccentricities; and where is the man that has not? But such as they really were, they were amply redeemed by the manly qualities to which I have alluded. He was not, in the usual sense of the term—perhaps not in any sense—what we esteem a great man. It was not his fortune to control the destinies of States—to preside over the deliberations of Cabinets, or to direct the movements of armies. Nor was he one of those—to use Mr. Macauley's fine expression in reference to Lord Holland—"who move great assemblies by reason and eloquence—who put life into bronze and canvass, or left to posterity things so written as it shall not willingly let them die." He did none of these things. His sphere of usefulness and field of action was of another, perhaps of a humbler kind, and his labors and exertions assumed a humbler form. Yet the great and beneficent results which he, and such as he, helped to accomplish, no man is yet able to estimate. He belonged to that race of men who laid the foundations of the Republic upon the principles of truth and justice—a race whose industry, enterprise and energy subdued the primeval forests—opened the great rivers of the continent—traversed the savannahs of the South and the prairies of the far West—who enlarged the boundaries of our country and planted its outposts beyond the summits of mountains. These were the conquests in which Mr. POWELL and his cotemporaries bore a conspicuous part—conquests that caused no tears, that cost no blood, and that inflicted no suffering, for they were the conquests of peace and christian civilization.

He had not the advantages of a liberal education. The knowledge derived from books, and taught at the schools, was denied him, for his youth was long past ere we perfected that system of public instruction which sends the schoolmaster into every hamlet, and places education within the reach of all. But his native sagacity, his powers of observation, his constant and close intercourse with the best business men of his time, more than supplied the place of early instruction. Whatever he achieved was due to himself alone. His wealth, his undoubted influence, his position as a merchant, a banker and a man of business, was due solely to his own industry, energy and integrity. In a public meeting of his neighbors and townsmen, it were idle to speak of his public spirit, and the uses he made of his wealth during the last twenty-five years of his life. How he applied it, and what he did with it, is fresh in the recollection of us all. It is sufficient to say, that whatever measure of prosperity we now enjoy—whatever of activity pervades our public streets, our workshops, our wharves and places of business, we owe to the prompt and intelligent interposition of Mr. Powell's wealth and credit between us and the legitimate results of great public improvements, which threatened to dry up the sources of our prosperity, and divert the streams of our business into other channels. He was not alone in his exertions to arrest the downward tendency of our prosperity. There were others, and especially one other, whose efforts were conspicuous in the same emergency, and to whom the citizens of Newburgh owe a debt of gratitude which it will be difficult to pay.

There was one peculiarity in Mr. POWELL'S character which entitles him to honorable and grateful remembrance. The pride of wealth is the infirmity of ignoble minds. He had no such weakness. He was, without doubt, for many years, the richest man in all this portion of the State, yet the influence of his circumstances wrought no change in his habits and manners, or in his genial and kindly intercourse with his fellow-men. The simplicity and economy of his youth remained unchanged to the close of his life. He disdained the empty and idle display—the luxurious ease of the fashionable quarters of a great city. He chose rather to dwell in the country, upon the bank of this noble River, in sight of these lofty and beautiful Hills, and to dispense and distribute his wealth where it had been mainly acquired, in the employment of labor, in the navigation of the River, the construction of Roads, the improvement and embellishment of his property, and in the mercantile enterprises of the firm of which, at the time of his death, he was the senior partner. It was true that his house was for many years the abode of a generous, and, I may add, a refined hospitality, but it was dispensed without the pride of wealth, or the ostentation of affluence.

In all my intercourse with Mr. POWELL, I ever found him a just and an upright man, and ever ready to recognize and respect the rights of others. He was fearless and resolute in the expression of his opinions—never concealing his disapprobation of what he deemed to be wrong, and his appreciation of what he thought right. Concealment and dissimulation was no part of his nature. He had a cheerful as well as a resolute temper of mind, never dismayed by defeat or turned aside from its objects by disappointment ; and he never lost that buoyant and exuberant spirit which was one of his chief characteristics. Even during the various illnesses which cast a shadow over his later years, this happy disposition did not leave him. I well remember being consulted by him some years since upon the final disposition of his estate. He was then confined to his house by an illness which he thought he could not survive. The interview lasted some time, and as I arose to take leave of him, I ventured to inquire if the near approach of death inspired him with any terror. He replied, with his usual cheerfulness: "Not in the least. I have long contemplated that event, and am quite prepared for it. I have outlived my capacity for usefulness and enjoyment, and have no longer a wish to remain. I regard death," said he, "as a necessary as well as an inevitable event, the consummation and completion of the state of being which we call life; and I shall encounter, without apprehension, and not without hope, the change which awaits us all."

It was, indeed, true, as he said, that he had outlived his ability to be useful, for he was well stricken in years and the infirmities of age were upon him. It is equally true, however, that he left nothing which it was proper he should do, incomplete and unfinished. Long before he separated himself from business and ceased to take part in its concerns, he had filled the measure of his usefulness, and executed the duties and trusts which his position imposed upon him with scrupulous fidelity and care. He descended into the grave full of years and not without honor—with little to regret in the past and much to hope for in the future—deplored by all who enjoyed his acquaintance—mourned by those who had the happiness to share his friendship.

It remains for those present to say what action they will take in regard to his memory.

On motion of Mr. CORNWELL, the Chair appointed the following Committee to prepare Resolutions giving expression to the sentiments of the Meeting: Messrs. D. W. BATE, GEORGE CORNWELL, JOHN J. MONELL, SAML. W. EAGER, HENRY WALSH, and SAML. J. FARNUM.

The Committee reported the following Resolutions:

1. *Resolved,* That the Village of Newburgh has suffered an irreparable loss in the death of THOMAS POWELL, its oldest, most prominent and useful citizen

—who directed his energies, his large wealth, unquestioned credit, and so many years of his life, in building up the business of this place—in projecting and completing the works of improvement which have established its present, and secured its future, growth and prosperity.

2. *Resolved,* That his absence of ostentation in his intercourse with society, in the midst of wealth—his industry, care and prudence, joined with an extensive liberality—identified, as he has been, for more than half a century, with the affairs of Newburgh, have done much to form the character and reputation of our people at home and abroad.

3. *Resolved,* That having risen from poverty to wealth, by the slow and usual channels of trade and business, he exhibited in his advancing years a rare and beautiful trait of character, by not hoarding his wealth for purposes of accumulation, but laying it out to surround his home—the abode of genial hospitality—with so many comforts and improvements; by bestowing so much of his property, during his life, where he might see others enjoy its advantages; and in expending it

so freely in works of enterprise, for the benefit of his fellow-townsmen.

4. *Resolved*, That we sincerely sympathize with his bereaved family under this afflictive dispensation, trusting that He who afflicts—not willingly—will, in His own good time, pour into their wounded hearts the balm of His consolation.

5. *Resolved*, That a copy of the proceedings of this meeting be signed by the officers thereof, and presented to the family of the deceased.

Hon. THOS. MCKISSOCK, in moving their adoption, said:

Mr. CHAIRMAN:—There is nothing presents a more beautiful exhibition than the expression of gratitude; and the exercise of that virtue is also highly beneficial to the subject of it, whether it be a person or a community. But this is especially so, when a just tribute of respect is rendered by the public to a benefactor. It is a great mistake to suppose that the love of praise does not move noble minds. On the contrary, it is a strong incentive to action in those of a generous nature, and even the selfish are often prompted to liberality by its incitement. It is, therefore, as I for the present assume, both profitable and respectful, that the people of Newburgh acknowledge the debt of gratitude they owe our deceased fellow-townsman, Mr. THOMAS POWELL, by offering the tribute to his memory contained in the resolutions just read.

Some places, like some persons, enjoy one uniform flood-tide of prosperity, while others are subject to the vicissitudes of success and sharp adversity. The latter has been the fortune of Newburgh. For a while she enjoyed, besides the business from the more immediate neighborhood, the trade from the interior as far west as the minor Lakes of the State. This was turned to good advantage, and had built up a thriving Village, when first the Erie and next the Delaware and Hudson Canal, like the approaching trenches of a beseiging army, straitened her limits and cut off her resources, till, if want and starvation did not absolutely stare the inhabitants in the face, yet it was perfectly plain, that unless a favorable change took place—of which there appeared little or no hope—many of the citizens would be compelled to seek some more fortunate place of business.

At this time, Mr. Powell had arrived at that age when most men, whether successful or unsuccessful in business, either retire or are thrust from active pursuits. Beside, he had retired on an ample fortune for those times and this region, counting his wealth at least by hundreds of thousands. After things had grown worse and worse, for some years, under the influence of the causes above mentioned, Mr. Powell, about the year 1835, stepped down from his peaceful retirement, and put his fortune again into the chances of business in Newburgh, the place where he had made his wealth. He had no son, and no child but one—now Mrs. Ramsdell—and but two grand-children, both girls, and could not, therefore, have been moved by the impulses of vigorous manhood, the suggestions of mercenary ambition, or the claims of domestic relations or family settlements, or the hope of gain, for we have just showed there was little hope of that here. What motive, then, can it be fairly presumed, moved him to this course? We answer, a manly, courageous, generous resolution to identify himself, for better, for worse, with the fortunes of the place where he had spent the better portion of his life, where he had married his wife, and where his children were born. And then an old man, he commenced a new career, that terminated only with his life, which was, fortunately for Newburgh, prolonged for nearly a quarter of a century.

He constructed wharfs and store-houses—built steamboats, under the charge of a most skillful agent, sparing no expense to make them of the very best class, for strength, accommodation and speed. At a cost of some $130,000, he established a ferry here, which has not been surpassed or even equalled on this river, except in or about the Port of New York.

Shortly after this, he associated himself with a few enterprizing and zealous men of the place, to construct the Hudson and Delaware Railroad, and when that enterprise was crushed out by the disasters of 1837, he and they stood firm to their purpose, if possible, to resuscitate the suspended animation of the place. For this, an opportunity shortly occurred. The New York and Erie Railroad, in progress of construction, was calculated to cut off the trade of the north-west portion of New Jersey and the southerly part of the County of Orange, which then still came to Newburgh. That Company became insolvent, and after lying in that condition for some time, a band of enterprising and generous men of the City of New York, having in view the noble purpose of increasing the commercial prosperity of that place, applied to the Legislature for certain privileges and immunities, to enable them to renew that work. The noble few in Newburgh saw in this the last chance to save the place, and accordingly they immediately set on foot a plan, if possible, to procure for the New York and Erie Railroad Company what they desired, but only on the condition that they should construct a Branch of their Road to Newburgh. An Act was passed embracing both these propositions, with another condition, that the people of Newburgh should subscribe for the stock of the Company one-third of all that was necessary to construct the Branch; or there was an agreement to the effect of this latter condition between the Railroad Company and the managing men of this place. Whether this latter condition was contained in the Act, or in an agreement as before stated, I am not positively informed.

Mr. POWELL now came forward, among the foremost, and subscribed for a large share of the stock which was agreed upon as the portion to be taken by Newburgh, as I have before stated. The stock was then much below par, with little or no chance of becoming par for a long time to come.

By the Act of the Legislature which I have referred to, the Company were bound to finish the Branch by or in the year 1851; but an earlier completion was highly desirable. And at this juncture, the Director of the Erie Railroad from this place—to whose talents, industry and indomitable perseverance this place is so largely indebted—procured a resolution of the Board of Directors of the Company, that if Newburgh would raise one-third of the money necessary for the immediate completion of the Branch (the whole being between three and four hundred thousand dollars), they would finish it without delay. Mr. POWELL, with several other of our citizens—he being best known and of the highest credit—(and without whose well-known responsibility it may, I think, be safely said, these operations could not probably have been effected)—gave their obligations for the amount, on which the money was raised, and the Branch was finished and put in operation the last of the year 1849.

I think it proper here to mention the name of another citizen of this place, now deceased, whose mind and best exertions were constantly devoted to the promotion of all plans calculated to advance the public interests, and who was always among the foremost in seeking the advancement of the schemes of internal improvement above referred to. It is scarcely necessary to say that I refer to Mr. John Forsyth.

On the day of the completion of the Branch Road, the prosperity of this place was set on a sure foundation. New branches of business have sprung up. The trade in lumber alone may be mentioned as one of great extent. That article of commerce is now sent from this place to New York, New England, New Jersey, Philadelphia, Baltimore, Washington City, Rio

Janeiro, Valparaiso, San Francisco, Australia, and many other markets, near and remote. I have seen ships twice as large as not long ago could have been found in the City of New York, two at a time, lying at our wharves loading with lumber for the Pacific.

The building of cars, also, is extensively carried on, and ship-building has received a new impulse from the facility of procuring timber. The sound of the axe, the hammer and the saw, and other implements of the mechanic arts, are now heard where before all was silence and gloom; and, in fact, new life and energy have been infused into every branch of industry and business.

To all those who will say that Mr. Powell, and the other men who associated with him, sought only their own interest in these matters, there is one short answer—No ingrate ever yet failed to have what he thought, or pretended to think, a plausible excuse for his unthankfulness.

But there was another respect in which Mr. Powell was of great service to this Village. While it was always understood that he was liberal and generous in his household and family affairs, it was equally known that he avoided all expenditure for show or ostentatious display. He provided all things necessary to a generous hospitality—he had always horses, carriages and servants sufficient for a liberal enjoyment of a comfortable independence—yet it plainly appeared to all that the vanity of surpassing others, in these particulars, had no place in his mind. He considered industry and economy as cardinal social virtues, that he openly declared at all times, and he practiced what he preached. Every one who has observed the influence of the example of the rich in such matters, on the social condition of small and even large communities, will readily consent to the conclusion, that the deceased was of great service to the inhabitants of this place, in promoting among them habits of industry and economy; and no one will deny that our people are distinguished for their diligence in business, their economical habits and thrift. If, then, the deceased has contributed in any degree to the production of such a state of society, he was, in this, a public benefactor, and entitled to our gratitude.

I move, Sir, the adoption of the Resolutions just read.

Mr. JOHN J. MONELL, in seconding the motion, said:

Mr. CHAIRMAN: I propose to add but a few words to what has already been so appropriately said in relation to our departed friend. For more than half a century he has been one of our most prominent citizens; he has benefited us all by his enterprise, and encouraged us to activity in business by a life of successful industry.

In looking around this assembly, I see none of the companions of his youth. They have long since been numbered with the dead. Our middle-aged men, several of whom have been associated with him in business, and our young men, who have grown up under the influence of his efforts, have come together to pay a tribute to his memory. This is no formal ceremony. It is not occasioned by any accidental professional or official position heretofore occupied by the deceased. It is the spontaneous movement of his fellow-townsmen, prompted by a grateful remembrance of all that has been done for them by the principal founder of their place.

And is it really true, that THOMAS POWELL, so familiarly known even to our children, is dead, and that he will never again be seen in our streets and along our wharves? It is true that he has gone from among us, but he is not lost to us. The impress of his character, the results of his industry and energy, will ever remain; and besides, he placed his mantle, during his life, with his own hands, on the shoulders of one whom the citizens of Newburgh will ever love to honor for what he has already done for them.

The deceased was a remarkable man—remarkable for the age in which he lived; for the physical strength and mental faculties which sustained him till his death; for his absence of ostentation in the midst of wealth; and for giving up the love of money and the desire for accumulation, when most men become more grasping and penurious. Incidents illustrative of his character will be related by father to son while our town remains, for his name is identified with improvements which must ever contribute to its prosperity. He was nurtured in the days of the Revolution, and early breathed the spirit of the founders of our Republic. He always exemplified a love of political equality in his intercourse with society, and made himself a living example of what our free institutions have done for man. He arose through the ordinary course of trade and business by a road which all may travel, from poverty to wealth and influence. He established his position by individual effort, and acquired possessions which in other lands few obtain, except by tracing their title through a long line of ancestry, to the time when they were first seized by fraud and violence. In his early years, before religious and political liberty had been established, he had witnessed priestly oppression and aristocratic assumption exhibited by the enemies of his country; and he was then taught to denounce the one and despise the other. In later years, when he thought of former outrages upon personal rights and privileges, influenced by the force of early habit, he would sometimes denounce with a boldness that belonged to another age. But those who knew him well, can testify how much he really appreciated refinement and true excellence, how gentle was his disposition, and how liberal and charitable his views.

But I will not speak more of the deceased, except to make one statement in relation to his religious belief. In the last conversation I had with Mr. POWELL, he said, that "after years of anxious thought he had come to the conclusion that he could not atone for his own offences, and that he needed a mediator, and hoped for pardon through his merits." He further said, "that he always made it a point to examine his daily life, each morning and evening, and ask God for direction."

And now assembled to commemorate the memory of an aged deceased neighbor, are we not reminded that within a short period an unusual number of our oldest and best citizens have gone down to the grave. CHAMBERS, JOHNSTON, LAWSON, FORSYTH, POWELL, and others that I might mention, are no more. Surely

"The hand of the reaper
Took the ears that were hoary."

Increased responsibilities are thus thrown upon us, and it becomes us to meet them promptly like men, for death awaits us all, and may come sooner than we expect. Then, while the heavens are still above us, spanned by the bow of promise—while we have health and prosperity—let us remember that,

> "The boast of heraldry, the pomp of power,
> And all that beauty, all that wealth e'er gave,
> Await alike the inevitable hour—
> The paths of glory lead but to the grave."

The report of the Committee was then adopted unanimously.

On motion, the meeting adjourned.

JOHN. W. BROWN, Chairman.
E. W. FARRINGTON, Vice-Chairman.

C. F. BELKNAP, } Secretaries.
S. R. VAN DUZER, }

Family Register.

THOMAS POWELL—BORN 1769, DIED 1856—AND MARY LUDLOW—BORN 1785, WERE MARRIED 1802.

THEIR CHILDREN.

HENRY T. POWELL, — DIED 1834.

ROBERT L. POWELL, — MARRIED LOUISA A. ORSO.

THEIR CHILDREN.

FRANCES E. L.

MARY LUDLOW, — MARRIED I. S. FOWLER.

HENRIETTA, — MARRIED W. A. M. CULBERT, M. D.

FANNY POWELL.

JAMES A. POWELL, — DROWNED 1828.

JACOB POWELL, — DIED 1816.

FRANCES E. L. POWELL, — MARRIED HOMER RAMSDELL.

THEIR CHILDREN.

MARY LUDLOW,

FRANCES JOSEPHINE, — MARRIED MAJOR G. W. RAINS, U. S. A.

THOMAS POWELL,

JAMES A. POWELL,

HENRY POWELL,

HOMER STOCKBRIDGE,

LEILA RAINS.

www.ingramcontent.com/pod-product-compliance
Lightning Source LLC
LaVergne TN
LVHW021423110826
845150LV00007B/2056

9781425510398